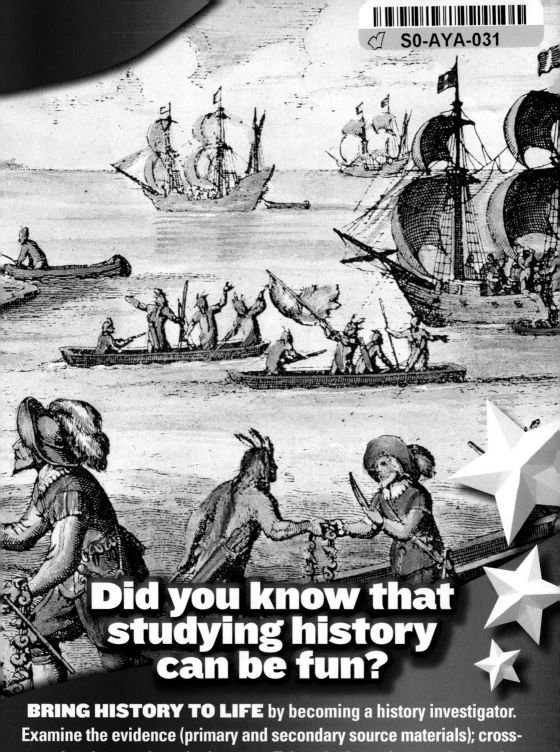

Did you know that studying history can be fun?

BRING HISTORY TO LIFE by becoming a history investigator. Examine the evidence (primary and secondary source materials); cross-examine the people and witnesses. Take a look at what was happening at the time—but be careful! What happened years ago might suddenly become incredibly interesting and change the way you think!

Contents

4

The JAMESTOWN COLONY

BY PETER BENOIT

CHILDREN'S PRESS®
An Imprint of Scholastic Inc.
New York Toronto London Auckland Sydney
Mexico City New Delhi Hong Kong
Danbury, Connecticut

BRINGING HISTORY to LIFE

Content Consultant
James Marten, PhD
Professor and Chair, History Department
Marquette University
Milwaukee, Wisconsin

Library of Congress Cataloging-in-Publication Data

Benoit, Peter, 1955–
   The Jamestown Colony/by Peter Benoit.
      p. cm.—(Cornerstones of freedom)
   Includes bibliographical references and index.
   ISBN-13: 978-0-531-23058-9 (lib. bdg.)
   ISBN-13: 978-0-531-28158-1 (pbk.)
   1. Jamestown (Va.)—History—17th century—Juvenile literature.
2. Virginia—History—Colonial period, ca. 1600–1775—Juvenile literature.
I. Title.
   F234.J3B45 2012
   975.5'02—dc23   2012000492

1 2 3 4 5 6 7 8 9 10 R 22 21 20 19 18 17 16 15 14 13

Photographs © 2013: age fotostock: 44 (Everett Collection Inc.), 11 (The
British Library); AP Images/North Wind Picture Archives: 6, 32, 36, 37, 42,
48; Bridgeman Art Library/National Geographic Image Collection: 35; Getty
Images: 40 (Archive Photos), 13 (F. Hinshewood/John G. Chapman/Kean
Collection), back cover, 47 (MPI); iStockphoto: 34, 57 bottom (Christopher
Paquette), 26 (pixonaut); Library of Congress: 5 bottom, 15 (Griffith Baily
Coale/Frank J. Raymond), 5 top, 10 (The Kraus Collection of Sir Francis
Drake); National Geographic Stock/Ira Block: cover; National Park Service/
Sidney King/Colonial National Historical Park: 18, 25, 46, 58, 59; North Wind
Picture Archives: 14, 22, 30, 39, 41, 56; Superstock, Inc.: 51 (Image Asset
Management Ltd.), 4 bottom, 12 (The Art Archive), 17, 28, 57 top (Universal
Images Group), 16 (Visions of America), 4 top, 20; The Granger Collection: 2,
3, 8, 27, 31, 50; The Image Works: 55 (Alonzo Chappel/akg-images), 23 (BeBa/
Iberfoto), 38 (Print Collector/HIP), 7 (TopFoto).

Maps by XNR Productions, Inc.

The Journey Begins

Spanish explorers successfully colonized the Americas in the 1500s.

In the bitter chill of December 1606, a hopeful group of men and boys rose from their sleep in Blackwall, England. Their minds were filled with dreams of land, gold, and adventure. They tried to imagine what the distant shores of Virginia, in North America, might look like. England's

Spanish rivals had grown wealthy in the Americas. The Virginia Company imagined similar success across the ocean when it decided to start a settlement of its own in North America.

The Virginia Company carefully weighed the risks of the new venture. A former British colony at Roanoke, in what is now North Carolina, had mysteriously disappeared in the late 16th century. The Powhatan Indians had quietly extended their influence throughout the Chesapeake Bay region to the north of Roanoke. Despite these challenges, the lure of wealth and fame filled the heads of the adventurers as they made their way to the three waiting ships. One year later, nearly two-thirds of them would be dead.

The story of Jamestown is one of astonishing courage and unimaginable suffering. It is also one of big dreams and major disappointments. But most of all, it is the beginning of America as we know it today.

British settlers arrived at Roanoke in 1587.

COLONY HAS NEVER BEEN SOLVED.

CHAPTER 1

THE LONG VOYAGE

Bartholomew Gosnold met and traded with Native Americans on his expedition to Cape Cod in 1602.

BARTHOLOMEW GOSNOLD

understood the challenges of **colonization**. Gosnold was an English lawyer and explorer who had led an expedition to Cape Cod in 1602 and established a short-lived colony there. He had also had earlier successes as a **privateer** and adventurer. This background made Gosnold the perfect candidate to plan a new English settlement in the Americas.

The Best-Laid Plans

Future colonist Richard Hakluyt had written a great deal about the benefits of English colonies in the Americas. He believed that England stood to gain in trade and natural resources. Overseas colonies would extend the influence of the English crown. They would also lessen the pressures of a growing population at home. The promise of new land was attractive to both gentlemen and laborers.

English laws dealing with **inheritance** of property made it unlikely that anyone with an older brother would become a landowner. Some of the Jamestown settlers, including Bartholomew Gosnold, had older brothers. Other colonists were religious leaders who saw an opportunity to bring Christianity to the native people of Virginia.

Several of Jamestown's first settlers were Gosnold's friends,

THE PRINCIPAL NAVIGATIONS, VOIAGES, TRAFFIQVES AND DISCOueries of the English Nation, made by Sea or ouer-land, to the remote and farthest distant quarters of the Earth, at any time within the compasse of these 1500. yeeres: Deuided into three seuerall Volumes, according to the positions of the Regions, whereunto they were directed.

This first Volume containing the woorthy Discoueries, &c, of the English toward the North and Northeast by sea, as of Lapland, Scrikfinia, Corelia, the Baie of S. Nicolas, the Isles of Colgoiene, Vaigatz, and Noua Zembla, toward the great riuer Ob, with the mighty Empire of Russia, the Caspian sea, Georgia, Armenia, Media, Persia, Boghar in Bactria, and diuers kingdoms of Tartaria:

Together with many notable monuments and testimonies of the ancient forren trades, and of the warrelike and other shipping of this realme of England in former ages.

Whereunto is annexed also a briefe Commentarie of the true state of Island, and of the Northren Seas and lands situate that way.

And lastly, the memorable defeate of the Spanish huge Armada, Anno 1588. and the famous victorie atchieued at the citie of Caliz, 1596. are described.

By RICHARD HAKLVYT Master of Artes, and sometime Student of Christ-Church in Oxford.

Imprinted at London by GEORGE BISHOP, RALPH NEWBERIE and ROBERT BARKER. 1598.

Richard Hakluyt wrote detailed accounts of the successful voyages and discoveries of English explorers in North America.

Sir Thomas Smythe helped finance the Virginia Company using money he had earned running a trading company.

relatives, and neighbors. Gosnold was from the town of Suffolk in East Anglia, England. A large number of the first Jamestown colonists came from Suffolk. They included Gosnold's brother, Anthony, and a cousin. Sir Thomas Smythe of Kent was another of Gosnold's cousins. He used part of his large fortune to help finance the project.

Dozens of settlers came from other English towns such as Essex and London. Some came from more distant locations. They held meetings at Otley Hall in Suffolk. Otley Hall was the manor house of Gosnold's

uncle. A manor house belonged to the nobleman in charge of the land. In addition to Hakluyt and Gosnold, privateer Christopher Newport of Essex, soldier John Smith of Lincolnshire, and Gosnold's cousin Edward Maria Wingfield of Huntingdonshire attended the meetings. Some settlers would be laborers who agreed to work for several years in exchange for transportation, food, and lodging. They were promised land in Virginia at the end of their service.

King James I granted the settlers permission to establish a colony in Virginia.

King James I established the Virginia Company by royal charter on April 10, 1606. The Virginia Company's three ships set sail from Blackwall little more than six months later.

The Voyage Begins

The largest of the three ships was named the *Susan Constant*. It was packed with supplies and heavily armed. The 76-foot (23-meter) ship was captained by Christopher Newport and carried 71 people. The *Godspeed* was under the command of Bartholomew

Christopher Newport (holding crown), the captain of the *Susan Constant*, was an important leader in the early days of the Jamestown Colony.

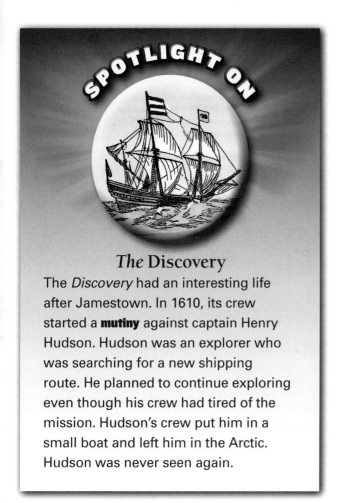

The Discovery

The *Discovery* had an interesting life after Jamestown. In 1610, its crew started a **mutiny** against captain Henry Hudson. Hudson was an explorer who was searching for a new shipping route. He planned to continue exploring even though his crew had tired of the mission. Hudson's crew put him in a small boat and left him in the Arctic. Hudson was never seen again.

Gosnold. It was smaller than the *Susan Constant* and carried 52 men. The smallest ship was the *Discovery*. John Ratcliffe was the captain. The *Discovery* carried supplies, equipment, and an additional 21 men.

In all, the party of adventurers numbered 144 men and boys. Forty of them were the ships' crews. The remaining 104 would be settlers in the new colony. There were no women. It seems certain today that there were no plans to settle down permanently in Virginia. The colonists thought only of the fame and fortune they could gain in the Americas. They hoped to find gold and a new passage to the South Sea, today known as the Pacific Ocean. Such a passage would speed trade with Asian nations, such as China and India. The settlers did have the means for creating a self-sufficient colony, though many of the colonists were gentlemen who were not used to hard work. They were poorly suited for the trials they would soon face.

The three Virginia Company ships and their crews experienced a difficult journey on the way to North America from Great Britain.

But other members of the party included five carpenters, a barber, two bricklayers, a mason, two surgeons, and a tailor. Skilled workers mixed with common sailors and boys.

The voyage was troubled from the beginning. The fleet was stalled helplessly near the mouth of the River Thames for more than a month as it tried to sail out of England. One storm after another pinned the three ships against the northern shore of Kent. Gosnold watched helplessly as the fleet's commanding admiral, Christopher Newport, was unable to get them on their way.

Gosnold must have wondered about Newport's abilities as captain when the fleet set sail toward the Canary Islands, off the coast of Africa, and then toward the West Indies,

Today, a replica of the *Godspeed* is docked where Jamestown was located.

in the Caribbean Sea. A more northerly route would have shortened the trip by several days. Gosnold's friend John Smith expressed his frustrations openly. Smith was a confident young adventurer who had served as a soldier in several conflicts in Europe. He was put in chains and charged with mutiny for speaking out against Newport. He would have been hanged if Gosnold had not stepped in. Tempers boiled over as the voyage stretched on for weeks.

In the Hands of Fate

Newport commanded the operation at sea. But no one knew who would lead the colony in Virginia. The names of those chosen for the governing council were sealed in a box. It was not to be opened until the party reached land. The Virginia Company decided to keep the colony's leaders a secret to ensure each adventurer's full commitment to the company's mission. Instead, the secrecy led men such as Smith to question the ability of men such as Newport and Wingfield to lead an expedition. Smith felt that leadership was something that had to be earned. He considered the poor decisions made by his superiors proof that they were not fit for the job. But many of these men found Smith to be young,

Many men of the Virginia Company thought that John Smith lacked the necessary skills to lead the colony.

The colonists knew that the voyage to North America was only the first part of a much longer struggle.

brash, and common. They believed that they deserved to lead because of their social standing. These differences would influence the colony in many ways.

When the ships stopped at Nevis in the Leeward Islands, Newport sent some of the men out to hunt and fish. Supplies had fallen dangerously low. He also asked some men to build gallows so he could hang Smith. Gosnold once again stopped Newport from hanging Smith. Smith was returned to chains and confined. But a division had formed among the adventurers. Smith said aloud what many others thought.

The three ships of the Virginia Company faced a far

more urgent problem within the next two weeks. They ran into a powerful and dangerous storm off the Virginia coast. It threatened to sink them or blow them off course. When the storm ended, the men were lost. But they were also very near the entrance to Chesapeake Bay. After many tense days afloat, the exhausted adventurers of the Virginia Company finally sighted land on April 26, 1607.

A VIEW FROM ABR★AD

Before Jamestown, England had not succeeded in establishing a permanent colony in North America. The Spanish crown had benefited greatly from this failure. Jamestown would change all of that. Documents issued by King Philip III of Spain in 1608 and 1609 indicate that he was concerned that Jamestown could become a harbor for pirates. He feared that these pirates would attack Spanish ships in the Atlantic Ocean.

The ships dropped anchor on the bay's south shore. The explorers went ashore and walked several miles inland. The tall trees and fresh waters of the location impressed them. A group of Native Americans attacked them on their way back to the ships. The colonists were able to fight them off, but a few suffered wounds. After weathering storms and avoiding shipwrecks and starvation, the men of the Virginia Company were reminded that other dangers lay ahead.

CHAPTER 2

THE TRIALS OF THE FIRST SETTLERS

After a long, rough voyage, the colonists were happy to arrive on the shores of North America.

SAFE ABOARD THE *SUSAN*

Constant, Newport opened the sealed box and read the names of the seven men chosen by the Virginia Company to govern the colony in its first year. It was not a surprise when the names of Newport, Wingfield, Gosnold, and Ratcliffe were announced. These men were all important to the expedition's organization. John Martin was not an unexpected choice either. His father was a major figure in London politics. George Kendall, another choice, was the cousin of a Virginia Company founder. He could be counted on to report accurately on the colony's progress. The last name on the list was more surprising. It was John Smith.

Compromise

Smith's position on the council divided the colony. It won Smith release from confinement, but Newport and Wingfield refused to seat Smith on the council. Others who felt they had a more reasonable claim to be seated were angry at not being included. Further confusion arose during the first weeks because the highest command was divided between Wingfield and Newport. Wingfield was the elected president, but Newport had been charged with leading the search for a suitable location to build the settlement.

Newport found that the Chesapeake's rivers could be navigated far inland. His search did not turn up any gold or a passage to the South Sea. However, the expedition met several groups of native people along the James River. Most were friendly and eager to trade. Eventually, a marshy **peninsula** was chosen for the settlement. The colonists named it Jamestown Island to honor the English king.

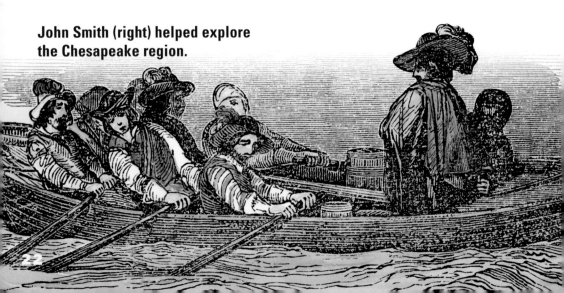

John Smith (right) helped explore the Chesapeake region.

The location of Jamestown Island had several advantages. The narrow land bridge at the western end made it easier to defend against attacks from native groups. The nearby channel was deep enough to bring the settlers' ships close to the shore. This made them easier to load and unload. Cannons could be used to protect the settlement if it was fired on from the river. Finally, the settlement would be nearly 60 miles (97 kilometers) inland from the coast. This would keep it far from the attacks of Spanish explorers. Satisfied that they had arrived at the best possible location,

YESTERDAY'S HEADLINES

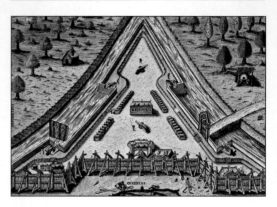

The decision of where to build Jamestown Colony was made carefully. It took into account the dangers that the new English outpost would likely face. In 1565, the Spanish had massacred 350 Frenchmen. The attack was meant to drive off the French, who had established Fort Caroline (above) atop St. Johns Bluff near present-day Jacksonville, Florida, the previous year. The Jamestown colonists knew that their settlement needed to be easily supplied and far enough from the coast that it would not attract the attention of the Spanish.

the colonists unloaded the ships, pitched tents, prepared the soil for planting crops, and began fishing. Some quickly built a brushwood fence for protection.

A FIRSTHAND LOOK AT
JAMES FORT

Much of what we know today about James Fort comes from the writings of George Percy and William Strachey. The painstaking work of archeologists has also unearthed important information about the fort. See page 60 for a link to see a photo of the fort's remains.

A Stern Test

Newport feasted with friendly native people as he continued his expedition inland. At the same time, a few hundred other native people tested the colonists' abilities by attacking the new settlement. Survivors quickly became convinced of the need for a more substantial fort. They began building it at once. The new fort was roughly triangular in shape and larger than the first. It had strong **palisades** 14 feet (4.3 m) high.

But Native American attacks were only one of many problems faced by the settlement. Mosquitoes were seemingly everywhere and carried a deadly disease called malaria. The small peninsula had a limited supply of game. Once hunting had cleared it out, the colonists would have to venture into the wilderness where Native Americans waited. The colonists also lacked a good supply of clean drinking water. They instead drank water that was salty and contaminated with germs.

During the early months of the colony, Virginia experienced the worst drought the area had seen in more

Colonists searched the area for food, water, and other supplies they needed to survive.

than eight centuries. Colonists grew thirsty working at a fast pace in the heat. They drank whatever water they could find. This water was often diseased and taken directly from the river. Illnesses such as dysentery, typhoid, and salt poisoning threatened to destroy Jamestown. By August 1607, food supplies were running dangerously low. The season for sturgeon and sea crab had passed. With no fish, the men had to rely on the "common kettle." This soupy meal was made from barley

TODAY'S PERSPECTIVE

It has long been recognized that starvation, typhoid, dysentery, and malaria all plagued Jamestown in its first years. August and September 1607 were marked by almost daily deaths. We now know that disease was not the only problem faced by the early Jamestown colonists. Historians today have come to better understand the role that drought may have played in those difficult times. Studies of tree rings from the time period show that temperatures were high and that there was little rain between 1606 and 1612.

and wheat boiled in water. It was often infested with germs and insects. Half of the 104 men and boys who had arrived in May to colonize the area were dead by the end of September. Fewer than 40 of them survived through the winter.

Turns of Fortune

The Powhatan people were more than 13,000 strong in the early days of Jamestown. They could have easily destroyed the settlement if they wanted to. They may have seen Christopher Newport and several others leave on the *Susan Constant* and the *Godspeed* at the end of June 1607, and concluded that the colony was being abandoned. However, the Powhatan chose not to harm the colonists. The few colonists who remained were sick and had little chance of survival. They no longer traveled the waterways. This meant that they did not threaten Powhatan hunting grounds. The Powhatan helped the ailing colonists by supplying them with food.

Relations with the natives had taken a turn for the better. But arguments among the colony's leaders had grown worse. Bartholomew Gosnold, who had been the voice of reason in these arguments, was one of the many who died in August 1607. His death sent the colony into a tailspin. On September 10, Martin, Ratcliffe, and Smith declared Wingfield incompetent and removed him from office. Smith took over the day-to-day command of the fort. Wingfield was humiliated. He planned to return to England as soon as Newport returned from his voyage to get more supplies.

The Powhatan people saved the colonists from starvation by sharing food with them.

John Smith realized that developing a good relationship with the Powhatan Indians would help the Jamestown Colony survive.

Newport had sailed back to England, carrying a shiny metal he had found during one of his inland expeditions. However, he soon learned that it was not gold he had found, but worthless pyrite, or "fool's gold." Word spread through the London financial world. Investors began to doubt the value of the Jamestown Colony. They likely would not have resupplied the mission if they had fully understood the difficulties the settlers faced. Instead, Newport returned to Jamestown with supplies as well as new settlers on January 2, 1608. But the supplies were not enough to feed the new settlers, much less the original colony.

A fire leveled the fort shortly after the new settlers

arrived. Only three dwellings remained. The supplies burned in the fire. To help the colony recover, Newport and Smith set out to trade with the Powhatan.

Finding the Balance

Smith had built trust and mutual respect with the Powhatan chief Wahunsenacawh while Newport was away. He would claim years later that the chief's daughter Pocahontas had made her father spare his life. It is more likely that Wahunsenacawh wanted to trade with the English for copper and other goods. He also wanted the settlers to recognize his authority. Smith had adopted a policy of being fair, but firm, in his dealings with the Powhatan.

Fights with the Native Americans in the following months convinced John Smith that the Powhatan could not be fully trusted. This made the colonists more aware than ever that they must learn to supply all of their own food. Because the colony's gentlemen contributed so little, they were a source of frustration to the laborers. With the prospects of a second supply uncertain, Smith and a party of explorers set out on a journey to find gold. They found none, but did find plenty of animals to hunt. They also learned that there were many bands of Native Americans nearby.

The second supply mission arrived from Great Britain in October 1608. It brought another 70 settlers, including some skilled Polish and German craftsmen. It also included the colony's first two women.

In London, sponsors of the Virginia Company had heard that Spain might be planning an attack on the colony. However, the colony had so far not produced anything to warrant sending English warships to protect it. Newport now took up the search for gold and a route to the South Sea with greater urgency. He believed that England would protect the colony if it were considered valuable. But both Newport and Smith had been unsuccessful in the search for gold and the South Sea passage. Smith believed that the future of the colony lay not in gold, but in producing **clapboard**, pitch, and tar.

Women began arriving in Jamestown in 1608.

The colonists needed skilled workers to help construct buildings in Jamestown.

Newport had brought a letter from John Smith when he had returned to England for supplies. Smith had written that the Virginia Company's goals of finding gold and a route to the Pacific were unrealistic. He requested that they instead send carpenters, masons, gardeners, and blacksmiths. This would help the colonists build the settlement from the ground up. He spoke of the plentiful natural resources he had seen with his own eyes. Smith was uncertain what type of reaction the company's investors would have to his letter. But he had more immediate concerns. Winter was upon the colonists. Smith needed to make a deal with Wahunsenacawh to prevent the colonists from starving.

CHAPTER 3

JAMESTOWN AND POWHATAN RESISTANCE

Relations between
the colonists and
the Powhatan
became strained as
Jamestown grew.

WAHUNSENACAWH HAD

watched Jamestown's growth with concern. He wanted to expel the settlers from the area forever. But Powhatan warriors were no match for the guns, swords, and cannons of the Englishmen. Smith visited the Powhatan camp in January 1609. He found the chief unwilling to trade on the usual terms. Wahunsenacawh demanded English guns and swords in return for corn. He also requested chickens and the construction of an English-style home. Smith was willing to give him the chickens and the house, but not the weapons. Giving the Native Americans such weapons would risk the safety of Jamestown. Sympathetic Powhatans warned Smith that Wahunsenacawh planned to kill him, so he left quietly in the darkness.

Troubled Times

Pocahontas

Pocahontas may have played a role as large as that of any English colonist in the eventual success of Jamestown. She may also have saved John Smith's life when she was only about 11 years old.

In April 1613, she was captured by the British during the first Anglo-Powhatan War. She was held at Jamestown and used to bargain for the release of English prisoners being held by the Powhatan. During her year of captivity, she was treated respectfully and taught about the Christian faith. Pocahontas refused to return to her father. She married settler John Rolfe instead. They had a son named Thomas and traveled to England to promote the Virginia Colony in 1616. Pocahontas died in England in March 1617.

Smith resorted to threats and violence to bend the native people to his demands. Though he returned home the following month with food, he had damaged the relationship between Jamestown and the Powhatan forever. He had also weakened the source of his power in the colony. He was no longer the trusted go-between. In addition, he found out that he had been betrayed by a group of the colony's German **artisans** who had begun spying for the Powhatan in his absence.

Smith dealt directly with the threats of attacks by the Powhatan and starvation. He ordered the men to build another

The Jamestown colonists relied on farming to provide them with much of what they needed to survive.

fort across the James River, on a hill that gave a broad view of the land. He also had them plant about 40 acres (16 hectares) of corn. He created a policy requiring each colonist to either produce enough food to support himself or face starvation and banishment. This policy upset many of the colony's gentlemen.

At the same time, London investors began to see other types of promise in the colony. England's population was quickly increasing. Virginia's undeveloped wilderness seemed like a solution to the problem of overcrowding. Virginia Company governors began to look for artisans to complement the new English settlers.

Even the reports of "savages" provided a reason to expand the colony. A large Protestant settlement in Virginia would help place England's biggest religion on an equal footing with Spain's Catholic missions in the Americas. Plans were begun at once for a much larger supply mission.

Tensions between the colonists and the Powhatan sometimes resulted in violence.

Many Native Americans converted to the Catholic religion.

Dark Before the Dawn

The third supply mission carrying more than 500 colonists left England on June 8, 1609. Among them were many laborers and women. The **flagship** of the fleet was the *Sea Venture*. It was a large supply ship built especially for the purpose of delivering provisions to Jamestown. The *Sea Venture* was swept up in a terrible storm little more than seven weeks after setting sail. The storm lasted three days. The ship took on water and seemed certain to sink. After giving up all hope, the crew

The *Sea Venture* crashed into the rocky shore of Bermuda.

spotted the coast of Bermuda and ran the ship aground.

The *Sea Venture* was destroyed. It had been carrying most of the supplies and 150 passengers. The other eight ships all reached Jamestown by August 1609. The sudden appearance of so many new colonists, and so few supplies, created problems for Jamestown. The abrupt growth of the population made the food shortage more severe. It also attracted the attention of the Powhatan. They began a siege of James Fort and stopped all trade with the colony. With winter approaching, there was not enough food for the colonists and little hope of getting more.

Almost 90 percent of the colonists died that winter, most from starvation or disease. Those winter months were times of unimaginable suffering and despair. When the food supply was gone, the colonists turned to their horses and dogs for food. They ate rats and mice. Some may have even eaten their fallen comrades. They did

The colonists had to share tiny amounts of food among themselves during the winter of 1609 to 1610.

Colonist George Percy kept a record of the harsh starving months in his *Jamestown Narratives*. He wrote: "Then having fed upon horses and other beasts as long as they lasted, we were glad to make shift with vermin, as dogs, cats, rats and mice." As shocking as this may seem, recent archeological discoveries suggest that it is true. Bones from butchered horses, rats, dogs, and cats have been found around the original Jamestown settlement. So have the remains of poisonous snakes. All were part of the colonists' diet during that desperate winter.

everything they could to stay alive.

Meanwhile, in Bermuda, the crew of the *Sea Venture* worked to build two small ships named *Deliverance* and *Patience*. They used pieces of the ruined flagship and cut down cedar trees for timber. When the two newly built ships reached Jamestown in May, only 60 colonists were still alive. These survivors decided to abandon the colony.

The colonists boarded the two ships to begin the voyage back to England. On their way out, they met a fleet of ships, just arrived from England, on the James River. The fleet was captained by Thomas West, Baron

Baron De La Warr's (kneeling) encounter with the fleeing Jamestown colonists prevented them from abandoning the settlement.

De La Warr. He ordered the fleeing settlers to return to Jamestown. The *Patience* was sent to Bermuda to gather food. With ample food supplied by De La Warr's fleet and the returning *Patience*, the colony was able to expand in the next year. Increasing numbers of women and children came to Jamestown. John Smith was injured in 1609 when his bag of gunpowder exploded. He sailed for England to seek treatment and never returned to Virginia.

CHAPTER 4

SURVIVAL and GROWTH

The incredible success of Jamestown's tobacco crops led to a rapid increase in the colony's population, as people came for a better life.

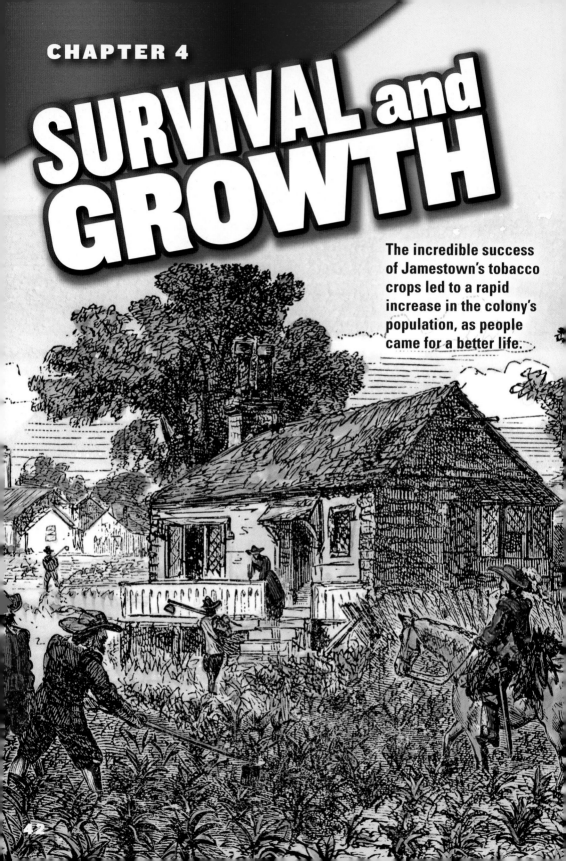

THE YEARS FROM 1611 TO 1624 were ones of major change for the English colonists in Virginia. The colonists witnessed the expansion of the original colony and the formation of a new settlement. They also saw the arrival of many single women and the region's first Africans, as well as the rise of representative government. The colonists' relationship with the Powhatan remained tense and ever changing. One of the biggest changes of this period was the success of tobacco as a **cash crop**. It stoked the dreams of investors and captured the attention of the British crown.

John Rolfe changed Jamestown forever with his Orinoco tobacco seeds, which produced an appealing tobacco that became a popular export.

Tobacco

Jamestown had been an economic disappointment before 1611. The original settlers' failure to find gold and their struggles to survive did little to encourage investors. Only the Crown's promise of expansion kept the Jamestown experiment from collapsing altogether.

The original investors were given 100 acres (40.5 ha) of land for each share of stock purchased. But Jamestown was on the verge of a new age.

One of the passengers aboard the ill-fated *Sea Venture* was named John Rolfe. He brought tobacco seeds that changed Jamestown. A small amount of native tobacco had been exported previously, but it was not well received in Europe. The seed Rolfe brought from Bermuda was a different kind of tobacco. Rolfe began exporting his crop in 1612. Its pleasant taste made it very popular in Europe. Rolfe's success spurred others to begin growing the new tobacco. It also vaulted him to a position of importance in Virginia.

Expansion

When De La Warr fell ill in 1611, Sir Thomas Dale replaced him as governor of Jamestown. Dale proposed rebuilding Jamestown. The town was improved and expanded. Homes were built outside of the original walls of the colony.

Dale recognized the limitations of the marshy peninsula. He knew the colony needed more space and better drinking water. Dale gave some thought to establishing a new settlement upstream. He believed it would provide enough land to satisfy wealthy investors and growth opportunities for tobacco planters. The town of Henricus was established in 1611 to provide such opportunities. John Rolfe moved to the new town in April 1614, after marrying Pocahontas. The

YESTERDAY'S HEADLINES

The tobacco John Rolfe brought from Bermuda was different from the plant that was native to Virginia. Rolfe's tobacco, which he called Orinoco, had a better taste than the kinds grown previously in the colony. It quickly became popular in Europe. Other planters rushed to copy Rolfe's success.

The tobacco boom had unexpected effects. Expansion of the colony into the wilderness made land less expensive. Fewer Europeans were willing to work for other planters because they could now afford their own land. By the mid-1600s, this created a huge demand for **indentured** Africans to work the tobacco fields. Competition also drove the price of tobacco down. It soon became much less profitable to grow. Many planters began to grow wheat instead.

move gave Rolfe the opportunity to expand his tobacco plantation. The marriage also lessened the strain between Jamestown and the Powhatan. But the improvement in relations was only temporary.

The founding of Henricus was part of a larger pattern of expansion and settlement. This expansion was driven by the success of the new tobacco. Investors began to band together to create large tobacco-growing settlements called **hundreds**. Many hundreds sprang up along the James and its tributaries. Each eventually grew into a small town. By 1617, Virginia was exporting more than 20,000

The colonists had to construct new buildings as the settlement grew.

pounds (9,000 kilograms) of Orinoco tobacco each year. But this expansion brought colonists into conflict with the Powhatan. Their uneasy truce would soon erupt in violence.

A Representative Government

As Jamestown and other Virginia settlements grew in size and wealth, some colonists began to question their loyalty to England. Thomas Dale set down a collection of laws to address this issue in 1611. This strict code required colonists to be loyal and obedient to King James. Those who broke the code were punished harshly. Speaking out against either God or the king could result in death.

Dale's laws did not stop Jamestown from forming a local government of representatives. On July 30, 1619, a **legislature** of elected representatives met in the Jamestown church to set the minimum price for tobacco at three shillings per pound. They also discussed other important matters. This legislature would eventually grow to become the Virginia General Assembly.

Enslaved people quickly became an important source of labor for Virginia tobacco planters.

Meanwhile, the need for labor increased as more hundreds were established and plantations grew in size. In August 1619, the first enslaved Africans arrived in the Virginia Colony. The year 1619 also saw the arrival of nearly 100 unmarried women from England. It was hoped that their presence would make the colony more stable and settled.

The growth of representative government and the success of the tobacco trade concerned the English crown. King James I feared losing control of the colony. To prevent this from happening, he decided to get rid of the Virginia Company. It was declared **void** in 1624. Virginia and Bermuda were officially made part of the royal empire the following year. The colonies were now under direct control of the British government.

Years of Tumult

Wahunsenacawh died in 1618. By 1622, his younger brother Opechancanough had risen to power. Opechancanough planned to forcefully remove the

A FIRSTHAND LOOK AT
DALE'S CODE

Thomas Dale established a harsh set of laws for the Virginia Colony. They required obedience to God and King James. The laws reflect loyalty to homeland at a time when James I worried that the colony might gain too much independence. See page 60 for a link to read Dale's Code online.

Despite being warned about a coming Powhatan attack, many settlers were killed in the Jamestown Massacre.

English settlers from Powhatan lands. He led an organized attack on English settlements along the James River on March 22, 1622. Most of the settlements were caught off guard. Several communities, including Henricus, were destroyed. A Native American boy named Chanco was told to kill his employer, Richard Pace. Chanco saved many people in Jamestown by telling Pace of the attack. Pace alerted his neighbors. Still, almost 350 settlers died in the bloody one-day massacre.

The angry colonists wanted revenge. They falsely proposed peace with the Powhatan. Then, they poisoned 200 Powhatan and slaughtered another 50.

Though he was never proven guilty, a man named Dr. John Pott was likely the one who created the poison. The stunning events began a bloody decade of conflict between the colonists and the Powhatan. The colonists built a palisade several miles wide across part of the Virginia peninsula. It gave them a measure of protection against the angry Powhatan. But it was not enough to prevent a brutal attack in 1644.

Opechancanough was captured two years later. Peace treaties were at last signed between the Powhatan and the colonists. By the end of the century, the Virginia capital was moved from Jamestown to Williamsburg.

SPOTLIGHT ON

Williamsburg

In 1633, English colonists founded a new settlement in the middle of a great palisade being erected on the Virginia peninsula. Called Middle Plantation, it grew into the first significant inland settlement. In 1699, the capital of Virginia was moved there from Jamestown, and Middle Plantation was renamed Williamsburg, in honor of King William III of England (above).

Williamsburg became an important center of colonial culture. It was the site of Virginia's first newspaper and theater. It also played a major role in the protests leading up to the American Revolution. Today, the city is a popular historic site. Many tourists visit to see reconstructed versions of original colonial buildings.

What Happened Where?

James River

Jamestown The first settlers from the Virginia Company chose Jamestown's location because it was easy to defend and difficult to see from the coast. It was the capital of the Virginia Colony until 1699.

James Fort

Jamestown Island

James River Most early settlements in Virginia were built along the James River. Rich soil and a constant water supply made it a perfect location for growing tobacco and other crops.

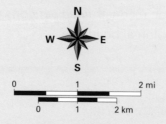

N
W · E
S

```
0        1        2 mi

0        1     2 km
```

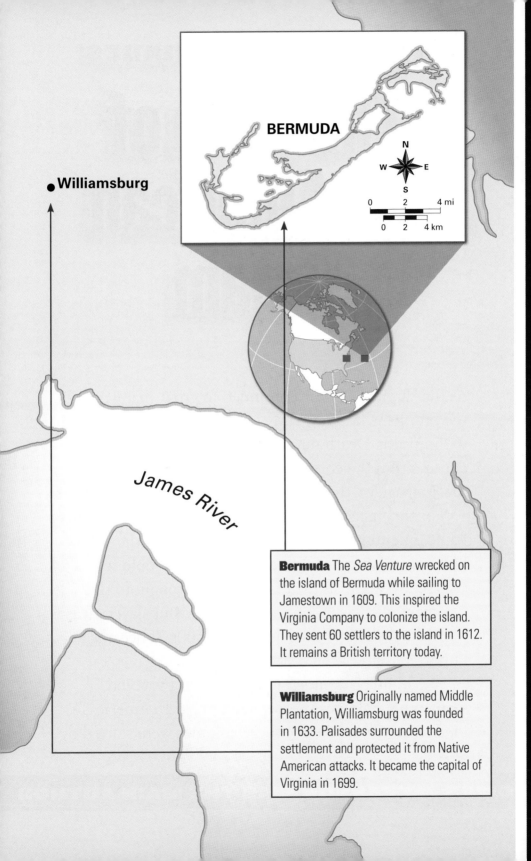

Williamsburg

BERMUDA

N
W   E
S

0   2   4 mi

0   2   4 km

James River

Bermuda The *Sea Venture* wrecked on the island of Bermuda while sailing to Jamestown in 1609. This inspired the Virginia Company to colonize the island. They sent 60 settlers to the island in 1612. It remains a British territory today.

Williamsburg Originally named Middle Plantation, Williamsburg was founded in 1633. Palisades surrounded the settlement and protected it from Native American attacks. It became the capital of Virginia in 1699.

The Birth of the American Dream

As the Virginia Colony continued to grow, many of the problems faced by early colonists slowly began to disappear. Death rates remained high for several decades. But the colonists pushed onward. Even with these struggles, they saw opportunity in the new land.

For the first several decades of the colony's existence, white indentured servants provided most of the labor. But as time went on, slavery began to take hold in the colony. Many of the first Africans brought to the colony worked as indentured servants. But slavery was fully established by the end of the 1600s. It became an important part of the colonial economy.

As Virginia continued to improve and succeed, many other colonies were created in North America. Like Jamestown, some of these colonies were started by

THOMAS JEFFERSON WAS THE MAIN AUTHOR

Great Britain. Others were begun by Spain and France. The British colonies came together in 1776 to declare independence from Great Britain and form the United States of America.

The 104 colonists who arrived in Jamestown in 1607 probably never considered the idea that their small settlement would one day grow into a great nation. Even though they came to America to find fame and fortune rather than to start a country, their efforts planted the seeds for the growth of the United States.

The Declaration of Independence officially separated the colonies from the rule of Great Britain.

Thomas West

Richard Hakluyt (ca. 1552–1616) was a well-known geographer. He wrote many works to convince people of the benefits of the English settling North America.

Opechancanough (ca. 1554–1646) was the younger brother and successor of Powhatan chief Wahunsenacawh. He hated the English settlers and planned the bloody massacre of March 22, 1622.

Christopher Newport (1561–1617) was a privateer and seaman. He led several supply missions to Jamestown.

Bartholomew Gosnold (1572–1607) was a leader in organizing the Jamestown expedition. He was also one of the original seven leaders of the colony.

Thomas West (1577–1618) was the 12th Baron De La Warr. He met the colonists leaving Jamestown and turned them back in June 1610. The state of Delaware, the Delaware River, and the Delaware Bay are all named after him.

John Smith (ca. 1580–1631) was a soldier, explorer, and author. He negotiated with the Powhatan and briefly led the Jamestown Colony.

John Rolfe (1585–1622) was a passenger on the ill-fated *Sea Venture*. He popularized Orinoco tobacco and married Pocahontas.

Pocahontas (ca. 1595–1617) was the daughter of Wahunsenacawh. She became an important bridge between the Powhatan and the Jamestown settlers. She married John Rolfe.

Wahunsenacawh (?–1618) was the Powhatan chief when the Jamestown Colony was established. He was a clever negotiator and the father of Pocahontas.

John Smith

Pocahontas

TIMELINE

1605–1606

Bartholomew Gosnold and others plan the exploration of Virginia.

1606

April 10
King James I charters the Virginia Company.

December
The *Susan Constant*, *Godspeed*, and *Discovery* set sail from Blackwall, England.

1607

May
Colonists establish the Jamestown settlement.

December
John Smith is captured by the Powhatan; according to Smith, Pocahontas saves his life.

1608

January 2
Christopher Newport returns from the first supply mission.

October
The second supply mission arrives and includes two women.

1612

John Rolfe begins exporting a new tobacco strain to England.

1614

John Rolfe marries Pocahontas, beginning a brief period of peace with the Powhatan.

1619

The first African indentured servants arrive in Jamestown; an elected general assembly meets for the first time at a Jamestown church.

1622

March 22
The Powhatan massacre almost 350 colonists.

1609

June 8
A third supply mission leaves England.

July
The *Sea Venture* runs aground on the coast of Bermuda.

August
The remaining ships of the third supply mission reach Jamestown.

1609–1610

Winter
Jamestown's population drops to 60 in what is later called "the starving time."

1610

May 24
The *Deliverance* and the *Patience* arrive and then leave for England with Jamestown's survivors.

June
Baron De La Warr meets the survivors on the James River and orders them to return to Jamestown.

1623

Colonists kill 250 Powhatan in revenge for the massacre.

1624

The Virginia Company charter is declared void.

1625

Virginia and Bermuda become Crown colonies.

1699

The Virginia capital is moved to Middle Plantation (Williamsburg).

LIVING HISTORY

Primary sources provide firsthand evidence about a topic. Witnesses to a historical event create primary sources. They include autobiographies, newspaper reports of the time, oral histories, photographs, and memoirs. A secondary source analyzes primary sources, and is one step or more removed from the event. Secondary sources include textbooks, encyclopedias, and commentaries. To view the following primary and secondary sources, go to www.factsfornow.scholastic.com. Enter the keyword **Jamestown** and look for the Living History logo **Σ¦**.

Σ¦ Dale's Code

Thomas Dale's rules were meant to keep the colonists in check when King James thought they were gaining too much independence.

Σ¦ The First Charter of Virginia

King James I signed this document April 10, 1606, granting the Virginia Company the rights to build a settlement in Jamestown.

Σ¦ James Fort

Archeologists have uncovered the ruins of James Fort. This structure helped to protect the Jamestown settlers during the colony's early days.

Σ¦ Smith's "Rude" Letter

In 1608, John Smith wrote a letter to the Virginia Company, asking them to reconsider their goals for the Jamestown Colony.

RESOURCES

Books

Carbone, Elisa. *Blood on the River: James Town 1607*. New York: Viking, 2006.

Lange, Karen E. *1607: A New Look at Jamestown*. Washington, DC: National Geographic, 2007.

McNeese, Tim. *Jamestown*. New York: Chelsea House, 2007.

Whiteknact, Sandra. *A Primary Source History of the Colony of Virginia*. New York: Rosen Central Primary Source, 2006.

Visit this Scholastic Web site for more information on Jamestown:
www.factsfornow.scholastic.com
Enter the keyword Jamestown

GLOSSARY

artisans (AHR-ti-zuhnz) people who are skilled at working at a particular craft

cash crop (KASH KRAHP) a plant that is farmed in order to be sold

clapboard (KLAP-bord) wood siding used to construct buildings

colonization (kah-luh-nih-ZAY-shun) the settlement of new land in order to place it under control of a foreign government

flagship (FLAG-ship) the main ship of a fleet

hundreds (HUHN-dridz) tobacco-growing settlements in colonial Virginia

indentured (in-DEN-churd) bound to work for a certain period of time in exchange for food, housing, transport from overseas, and land

inheritance (in-HER-uh-tuhns) money or property received from someone who has died

legislature (LEJ-iss-lay-chur) the part of government that is responsible for making and changing laws

mutiny (MYOO-tuh-nee) a revolt against authority, especially in the military

palisades (PAL-i-saydz) fences forming a defensive barrier

peninsula (puh-NIN-suh-luh) a piece of land that sticks out from a larger landmass and is almost completely surrounded by water

privateer (prye-vuh-TEER) an individual or a ship that is hired to attack enemy ships during wartime, but is not a part of the military

void (VOYD) not valid or legal

INDEX

Page numbers in *italics* indicate illustrations.

ABOUT THE AUTHOR

Peter Benoit is a graduate of Skidmore College in Saratoga Springs, New York. His degree is in mathematics. He has been a tutor and educator for many years. Benoit has written more than two dozen books for Children's Press. He has written about ecosystems, disasters, and Native Americans, among other topics. He is also the author of more than 2,000 poems.